SWAMI NITYANAND TEMPLES IN KANHANGAD & GURUVAN

• JOURNEY OF THE CHOOSEN ONE •

MONESH NAVNIT MEHTA

notionpress.com

INDIA • SINGAPORE • MALAYSIA

ISBN 979-8-89588-999-2

Contents

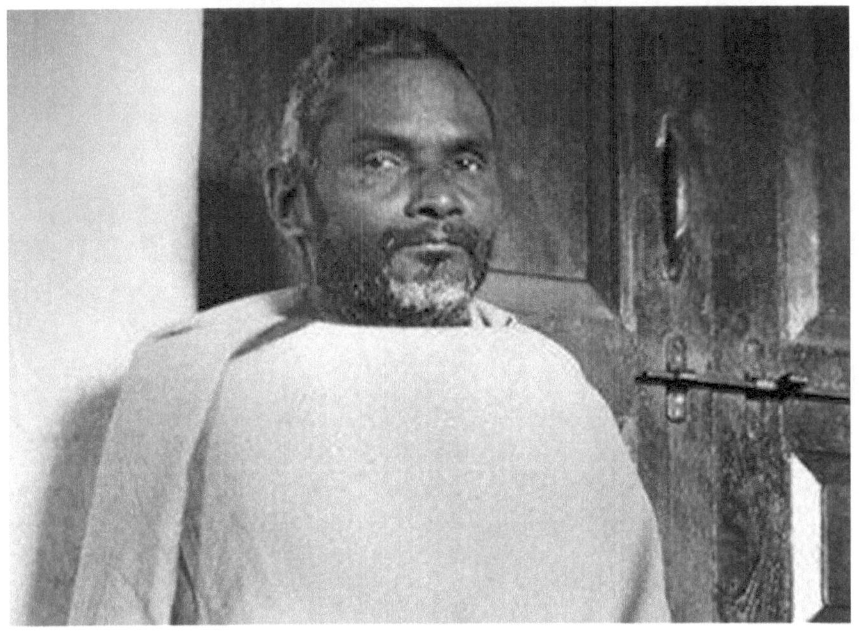

॥ ॐ ॥

गुरुर्ब्रह्मा गुरुर्विष्णुः गुरुर्देवो महेश्वरः ।

गुरुः साक्षात् परब्रह्म तस्मै श्रीगुरवे नमः ।।

॥ ॐ ॥

वक्रतुण्ड महाकाय सूर्यकोटिसमप्रभ ।
निर्विघ्नं कुरु मे देव! सर्वकार्येषु सर्वदा ।।

॥ ॐ ॥

कर्पूर गौरम करुणावतारं, संसार सारं भुजगेन्द्र हारं।
सदा वसंतं हृदयार विन्दे, भवं भवानी सहितं नमामि ।।

॥ ॐ ॥

या देवी सर्वभूतेषु शक्तिरूपेण संस्थिता
नमस्तस्यै नमस्तस्यै नमस्तस्यै नमो नमः

॥ ॐ ॥

कृष्णाय वासुदेवाय हरये परमात्मने ।
प्रणतक्लेशनाशाय गोविन्दाय नमो नमः ।।

॥ ॐ ॥

करचरणकृतं वाक्कायजं कर्मजं वा श्रवणनयनजं वा
मानसं वाऽपराधम् ।
विहितमविहितं वा सर्वमेतत् क्षमस्व जय जय करुणाब्धे
श्रीमहादेव शम्भो ॥

Preface

One day in the early 1990s while travelling from our office to home, on a local train in Mumbai, I told my brother, Keval, that I felt like I should write a book but at that time did not know on what subject.

After many years during one of my visits to Mumbai, I discussed with my family the idea that we should share with devotees around the world about how Dada devoted his time and efforts to building both the temples of his Guru Swami Nityanand in a small town of Kanhangad and the Guruvan area of Kerala state and dedicated them to the public.

Dada, as I remember, was forthright, sincere, family-oriented, and a successful businessman. He had great respect and admiration for his mother. Since I was his eldest grandson, he loved and pampered me the most, and sometimes, I miss him even today. Every morning he would sit in his room and have a traditional Gujarati breakfast with my Dadi, myself, and my younger brother.

He would feed the crows who would sit on the window panel every morning waiting for him to start his breakfast. After his morning chores, Dada would get ready and go to Papa's shop and before reaching the shop he would go to feed grass to the cows in Panjrapole and offer some sugar and jaggery mix to the ants at the base of the huge Pipal tree.

Dada would talk to us about different things. One morning as I was sitting next to him he said that as we are Gujaratis we would prefer to join our family business but he emphasised to me to get a commerce degree and become a graduate because he said 'we never know when our time would change, and a degree will be needed in the future', and that was the reason I graduated and this degree did help me at the time when it was needed.

This was an opportunity for me to write about the legacy of our family and dedicate a book to my Dada. The temple in Kanhangad completed 60 years in 2023, and in six decades four generations of devotees have become believers and seekers of Bhagwan Nityanand. We realised that over the years, facts about the temples have been distorted, and Itihas (history) must be corrected.

Dada had passed all the photo memories to my father, and we were fortunate to have a collection of photos from the time of the construction and Pranprathistha (consecration). We have tried to compile the facts and process, adding as many photos as possible to give the devotees the right perspective and a visual treat.

Through this book, I have tried to delve into the remarkable journey undertaken by 'Shri Babubhai Hargovindas Mehta–Lokhandwala,' who devoted himself to fulfilling the divine's mission.

My DADA & me

Om Nityananda

Disclaimer

We have tried our best to narrate (share) the events of the temples' construction and about Swami Nityanand and Jananand Baba's journey as accurately as possible. We are sure that all the details in this book are as per our collective memory; any chronological disorder is regretted. The repetition of a few sentences (events) was intentional.

We express our profound gratitude to all who have supported us in this noble endeavour, both directly and indirectly.

For further insight, an interview is available of Shri Navnit Babubhai Mehta speaking passionately about his father's unwavering devotion, which can be found on the YouTube channel 'Shifting into Awareness' (by Mr. Jacob, "Talk with Mehta family who built the temple of Kanhangad.….")

"Jai Nityananda" to All

From:

Shri Navnit Babubhai Mehta (Lokhandwala)

Smt. Jayshree Navnit Mehta

Mr. Monesh Navnit Mehta

Mrs. Deepali Monesh Mehta

Mr. Karan Monesh Mehta

Mr. Dhruv Monesh Mehta

Mr. Keval Navnit Mehta

Mrs. Kanan Keval Mehta

Ms. Niyati Keval Mehta

Chapter 1

Early Life of Shri Babubhai Hargovindas Mehta

On 13th January 1919, in the twin city of Savar-Kundla situated in the Saurashtra region of Gujarat state of Bharat (India), my Dada, Shri Babubhai Hargovindas Mehta was born. His parents, Shri Hargovindas Hansraj Mehta and Smt. Maniben Hargovindas Mehta had seven children—five sons and two daughters. Babubhai was the third child. Babubhai's father had a business of selling Indian sweets, and the livelihood of the house was taken care of from that income.

Babubhai's father owned a house and a sweet shop in Kundla village. Occasionally, he would give Babubhai four Annas (a currency from British India, equivalent to 25 paise today). Babubhai would then go to a nearby shop to get Gujarati food, and the whole family would sit together for dinner. The river Navli flows from South to North and divides the villages of Savar & Kundla, Savar is on the East bank, and Kundla is on the West bank of Navli.

Right from a very young age, Babubhai was sporty and playful and would swim in the Navli River. He had many friends on both sides of Navli. On Diwali night, people from Savar and Kundla come to the riverbank to throw handmade fireworks, called "Ingoriya," across the river. These fireworks are made by filling the fruits of the Ingoriya tree with explosives. Traditionally, this event is known as the cracker war, where two local cultural groups have a friendly competition. This tradition is still celebrated, till date.

Babubhai regularly went to a vyayamshala (gym) near his house. In those days, education was a luxury, so he studied up to the 4th standard at the village school, where he excelled in numbers. Babubhai was very ambitious and a seeker he wanted to explore and grow in life. He always thought big and wanted to achieve a better lifestyle for himself and his family.

Migration to Bombay!!

Babubhai's first attempt to go to Bombay was inspired by Gandhi's Non-Cooperation Movement against the British. One day he decided to go to Bombay to be part of the Non-Violent Satyagraha Movement. Without informing his parents he started his journey to Bombay with two other friends. Babubhai's father who cared for his children lodged a missing complaint with the local police station. The police from a nearby town found Babubhai, but his friends managed to escape and reach Bombay. Babubhai was then brought back to Kundla.

Couple of years later, Babubhai again thought of moving to Bombay, this time with the consent of his parents, to access more resources and to upgrade his and his family's lifestyle. In 1933, at the age of 14, he arrived in Bombay by himself, determined to succeed. He stayed in Bombay with his elder brother, who had arrived a few months earlier. Looking out for a job he was able to join an iron and steel merchant's company that was also from Gujarat having their office in Lokhand Bazar (Iron Market) in South Bombay for many years and he started earning a living.

He enjoyed his work and dreamed of the future. He soon called his siblings and his parents, and gradually the whole family got settled in Bombay. He worked for a few years with the company and learned the trade and business traits. He soon decided to leave his job and entered the iron and steel brokerage business, establishing contacts with other traders and manufacturers. Soon, Babubhai was a well-known name in the business community.

Over time, Babubhai's ambitions grew, leading him to start his own iron and steel business, achieving success at an early age. In 1942, he married Smt. Vimlaben Parekh who came from a prosperous family in Rajula, a village in Saurashtra, Gujarat. After the birth of his elder son Shri Navnit Mehta in 1944 Babubhai bought his own office in the Iron market. He partnered with a wealthy iron and steel merchant and imported steel from a Japanese company, which arrived at Bhavnagar port.

After selling the steel to the rolling mills in Gujarat, he continued in the trading business. As the ambition grew, within a few years he set up two rolling mills in Bhavnagar and owned a trading office also. He had the luxury of flying to Bhavnagar by aeroplane to do business & go on a vacation with his family and come back to Bombay by plane. Every year, Babubhai took a family vacation to religious cities in India.

Chapter 2

Family Life of Dada

Shri Babubhai and Smt. Vimlaben were blessed with three children: two sons and one daughter, Navnit, Arvind, and Niranjana. All three enjoyed a happy childhood because of their loving and supportive parents. Being the only girl, Niranjana was pampered by her parents and brothers. Babubhai's thriving business allowed him to own luxuries such as motor cars and even facilitated the purchase of a house in Bombay. All the five brothers and their families lived in the same building and on the same floor for many years. As time passed the children grew older and the brothers moved to different locations in Bombay and lived their lives and had their own business.

Babubhai always supported his children to study and finish their college education. He felt that because he did not know English it was difficult to communicate with the exporters overseas. So he asked his elder son Shri Navnit Mehta to draft letters in English for him and communicate with the suppliers. He supported both his sons to start their wholesale and retail shop selling stainless steel utensils in South Bombay.

Babubhai and Vimlaben shared love, respect, and a deep understanding. Vimlaben was intelligent and supported her husband in all his social, business, and spiritual pursuits. She loved her three children and her grandchildren equally. After his marriage, Babubhai always wore a white khaadi kafni, pure cotton white dhoti, a pure cotton starched white or black topi, and a cotton jacket—a status symbol of that time and to support the call by Gandhiji to use Swadeshi clothes.

Chapter 3

'Mother'

Babubhai deeply respected his parents, especially his mother, Smt. Maniben Hargovindas Mehta. He believed that her blessings played a big role in his success as a businessman and for his connections with well-known saints, including his guru, Shri Nityanand Baba.

In 1975, when his mother was about 93 years old, Babubhai honoured her with a special Tulabhar ceremony at their home in South Mumbai. This is an old Hindu tradition where a person is weighed against something valuable. For his mother, Babubhai chose pure silver bricks that matched her weight, which was around 40 kg. The event was a big occasion, with family, friends, and relatives gathered to celebrate. Babubhai wanted to show his gratitude to his mother in this special way, and the day brought everyone together in her honour.

*Smt. Vimlaben Babubhai Mehta and
Smt. Maniben Hargovindas Mehta (Babubhai's mother)
at the time of her Tulabhar*

Chapter 4

Spiritual Inclination

Sant Shri Gadge Maharaj

Babubhai was spiritually inclined and would take his small family to different places of worship a few times every year. He was an ardent devotee of **'Shree Lakshmi Narayan Bhagwan'** and would sit for long hours in deep meditation every evening in his house. There was a temple of Laxmi Narayan Bhagwan in the Bhuleshwar area of South Bombay where Babubhai would go daily to worship his Aradhye.

In the early 1950s, Babubhai came in contact with a renowned saint of Maharashtra, Sant Shri Gadge Maharaj, who was a Krishna bhakt. He was well-known for the mantra **"Gopala Gopala Devki Nandan Gopala,"** which he chanted during public kirtans. He was known for promoting personal well-being, cleanliness, and hygiene in different villages across the state of Maharashtra.

Gadge Baba was once a family man who turned Sanyasi because of a few life-altering events. He was detached from worldly pleasures and needs. He would not care about the kind of clothes he wore, the food he ate, or where he slept. He always wore a long cotton kafni with patches to cover the torn areas, and he wore socks of different colours and rubber slippers as his footwear.

Shri Gadge Baba used to visit Babubhai's house whenever he was in Bombay. He would ask Vimlaben for two annas for his tram fare, as Baba wanted to go to the JJ Hospital in the Mazgaon area and pay a visit to the patients and their relatives there. The great part about Maharaj was that if Vimlaben gave Baba four annas (currency at the time of the British), he would refuse and ask for only two annas, which was enough for his travel, otherwise, he warned her that he would go walking. (16 annas made 1/- Rupee.)

When Vimlaben offered Maharaj a thali of homemade Gujarati food, he would take all the varieties and mix the meal in a bowl (which was the bottom of an earthen pot) that he would wear on his head to protect himself from the sun. Then he would spill the same food on the floor, mix everything, and take the same food back in the bowl to eat.

Maharaj was very fond of Babubhai, and every time he came home, he would give blessings to him and his family. Maharaj had asked Babubhai to supervise the construction of the Gadge Maharaj Dharamshala, situated near J.J. Hospital in Mazgaon, Bombay. Babubhai also made a small donation contribution to the construction work.

One fine morning, Shri Gadge Maharaj came home to meet Babubhai. Maharaj was impressed with Babubhai's devotion and dedication to Lakshmi Narayan Bhagwan and himself, so he offered to grant Babubhai any wish he desired. But Babubhai very humbly informed Baba that he was grateful to God who had given him everything, and he would not like to have anything more from Baba. Baba repeated this sentence three times. When Babubhai shared the same intention with Baba, Maharaj slapped Babubhai on his thigh and made him promise never to ask anything from any God or saint again, regardless of life's circumstances. It seemed that Maharaj knew that soon Babubhai would find his enlightened guru, Nityanand Baba.

Before leaving, Maharaj put his hand on Babubhai's head and blessed him for life. Babubhai kept the promise for all his life.

That was the last time Sant Shri Gadge Baba met Babubhai before he took Samadhi. Gadge Maharaj's temple is in Amravati in Maharashtra.

After Gadge Maharaj's passing, there was a spiritual vacuum in Babubhai's life.

Sant Shree Gadge Maharaj

Chapter 5

Dada Meeting his Guru

Babubhai would sit for meditation for one to two hours every evening. He told me that he once entered such a deep meditative state that he couldn't return to normal. His craving to smoke a cigarette helped him come out of it, otherwise, it could have been fatal.

One evening during meditation, Babubhai had a divine vision of 'Lakshmi Narayan Bhagwan' asking him to make a guru, and showed a visual of the man who would be his Guru. Babubhai started wondering for the next few weeks how he could meet the man in the vision and accept him as his Guru.

One day, Babubhai took his family to Vajeshwari Mata's temple, a place of worship, 90 km from Bombay. His younger son, Arvind, fell off the car hood and suffered a serious injury that required medical attention. On inquiring, it came to Babubhai's knowledge that there was a doctor named Dr. Kothawala in the Ganeshpuri area, a couple of kilometres away from Vajeshwari.

After his son's treatment, Babubhai learned that a saint named Swami Nityanand lived nearby.

Babubhai went to Ganeshpuri the following Sunday to take the darshan of Nityanand Baba and meet him. Babubhai saw Nityanand and understood that he was the man in his vision.

When Nityanand Baba saw Dada standing at a distance, he looked at him and uttered the words, **"Hmm, Agaya?" (Hmm, you came?) "Jao Kund mai snaan karo phir nasta karke aavo"** (Go take a dip in the hot water springs bath and then have food and then come).

This is how a household devotee met his enlightened Guru.

Babubhai was lovingly called Lokhandwala Seth by Nityanand Baba as there were more than three Babubhai and also because he was in the Iron and Steel business. It was fate that had brought household devotee to his Guru.

On weekends Babubhai would visit Ganeshpuri. Babubhai enjoyed being in the presence of Bhagwan even though Baba did not talk at length, only a few words or in one sentence he would reply to the devotee's query. The connection between the two was growing stronger. It felt like something from his past life. Babubhai would take his family for Baba's darshan. It would become a picnic for his kids and his brother's children. There was a lot of positivity in the presence of Baba.

Baba enjoyed being around children and often gave them fruits and candies. Baba also said that one should offer food to children, poor and hungry rather than money because they know the importance of food compared to those whose stomachs are full.

He also said that if one offers money and if they do wrong things with that money then that person (giver) will be a supporter of that unlawful act and negative karma will happen to him/her also.

Every day, thousands of people would visit Ganeshpuri to take the darshan of Nityanand Baba and receive his blessings. Baba would always ask close devotees if they had taken a dip in the holy hot water spring bath nearby and if they had breakfast. It was said that during Brahma Muhurta many divine souls would come and take a dip in those hot spring baths.

When Nityanand Baba started staying in the Kailash building, he would take walks on the terrace where all the close devotees would stand and watch Baba's divinity. Sometimes Baba would also give prasad to the devotees.

Baba had asked Babubhai to stay in room no. 2 of the Kailash building which was adjacent to the terrace. Sometimes his wife and children would also join him and stay over the weekend.

Dada, (Grandfather) (Shri Babubhai Lokhandwala) met various prominent saints in his lifetime. First, it was Gadge Maharaj who came home to meet Dada and blessed him and his family. Because many saints came to meet Nityanand and some would stay around Bhagwan, Dada was Guru Bhai (devotees who follow the same Guru) with Jananand Baba, Kutiram swami, Shaligram swami, Govind swami, Sadanand swami, Mahabal swami, Muktanand Swami and a few more.

For 25 years, both before and after Baba's Samadhi, Dada consistently spent his weekends with his Guru.

Every Saturday morning Dada would drive to Ganeshpuri. His routine there was to take a bath in the hot water spring then go to Shri Kariya Shetty's Ramesh Bhavna restaurant to have breakfast and then go to have darshan of Baba near the hot water spring baths or in Kailash building. Dada would spend his time in the presence of Baba and do some official work that was given to him. After giving seva and after getting permission from Baba, Dada would go to the Kailash building and rest for the night where he had kept his bedding for many years as Baba had asked him to stay in one of the rooms whenever he came to Ganeshpuri. Sunday morning, he would stay in Baba's presence and by afternoon would take Baba's permission and leave for Mumbai.

In 1958 - 59 Nityanand Baba asked 10 men and 1 woman who were close devotees to go to Kanhangad, Kerala, and have a look at the cave work which he initiated and Jananand Baba had completed in 1931.

Baba called this group '**Dash Avatars plus Shakti**'.

As Dada was also part of the team, he was able to meet Jananand Baba for the first time in Kanhangad and there was a good connection between them.

Some of the devotees involved in the **Dash Avtaar** included **Babubhai Mehta Lokhandwala, Chimanbhai Parekh, Babubhai Gokani, Muktanand Swami, Maneklal Zaveri, Shankar Rao, Prahladbhai and his wife Umaben (as Shakti),** along with three others.

All 11 devotees travelled by Steamer ship owned by Scindia Steam Navigation Company to Mangalore and from there to Kanhangad by road.

In 1960, while taking rounds on Kailash terrace, Nityanand Baba informed Dada and other devotees who were present, that he had to leave his body by taking Mahasamadhi in Ganeshpuri. On inquiring why, Baba informed them that there was a message from the 'Sapta Rishis Mandal' (seven Brahma rishis) (Constellation of Ursa Major) for him to go back to them, as his time on Earth was over. He also informed them that there was going to be Aastha Graha Yuti (Eight planets were going to come in one line) and that would be a very tough period for the world.

In February 1962 the Aastha Graha (eight planets) came in line.

A few months before Mahasamadhi, Baba shifted his stay to the Bangalorewala building. It was said that Shri Laxmansha Khoday wanted Baba to visit his house in Bangalore, but Baba's body was too weak to travel so far. So, to fulfil Khoday's wish, he stayed in Bangalorewala building constructed by Shri Khoday.

One day, when Dada went to take Baba's darshan in the Bangalorewala building, Nityanand Baba showed a divine vision to Dada. There, Baba asked Dada if he wanted to have a darshan of 'Bal Krishna Swaroop' and asked him to look out of the window at a big tree that was situated on the right side of the pathway to the Tansa River. There, Dada saw Bal Krishna standing on the branches of the Pipal tree, playing his flute. Baba said that one who gets the opportunity to have Bal Krishna's darshan would not take any other birth. This divine vision was proof enough for Dada that Nityanand Baba was an Enlightened being himself.

On a certain day, Dada got a call from one of the devotees informing him that Baba was remembering him.

Dada knew this was going to be the last time he would be meeting his Guru and Bhagwan.

On 1st August 1961, which was Lokmanya Tilak's Jayanti, Dada arrived in Ganeshpuri. He took a dip in the hot water bath and quickly went to see Baba at Bangalorewala building, where Baba stayed until his samadhi. As he went to see Baba, one of the sevaks, Madhu mama, told him that Baba had been thinking of him and had been asking for a few days to 'call Lokhanwalaseth'. The sevak also mentioned that Baba asked them to report the amount of money collected and to bring it all to him, which was the most surprising behaviour for "Baba, the Avdhoot".

Dada went to meet Baba on the 1st floor of the Bangalorewala building. On seeing Dada, Nityanand Baba was very eager & happy and asked Dada to come near him and sit at his feet.

There, Baba gave him a Parcel that was wrapped in newspaper and asked him to go home and then open it. Baba said, "Keep this in your house and things will be taken care of". Gurudev also put his hand on Dada's head and moved it around in a circular motion thrice and blessed him for life and a few more to come. Dada stayed in Baba's presence for the day and then took Baba's permission to go back to Bombay.

This was the last time a Bhakt met his Guru in person.

While driving back home from Ganeshpuri Dada was sad but very anxious. On reaching home Dada called Dadi (Vimlaben) and his children Navnit, Arvind, and Niranjana who sat down to open the parcel. Dada and family were surprised to see that there was a Loin cloth that Baba used to wear which was filled with currency notes of almost all denominations with few coins including some small gold coins.

On 8th August 1961, Nityanand Baba took Mahasamadhi in the Bangalorewala building and became Bhagwan for his devotees.

In the Bhakti movement of India, saints and spiritual masters can be addressed as "Bhagwan" out of reverence for their spiritual attainment. This word is suitable for individuals who have realised their oneness with the divine.

Chapter 6

The Abhay Mudra Murti

Kanhangad was very dear to Nityanand Baba. The Kanhangad temple is believed to represent the Sahasrar chakra, while the Ganeshpuri temple represents the Muladahar chakra.

After Baba's samadhi, Dada went to Kanhangad a few times and stayed there for a few days with Jananand Baba's permission. There was an instant connection between them during his visit as part of the Dash Avtaar team.

On one such visit of Dada to Kanhangad after Nityanand Baba's samadhi, Jananand Baba informed Dada that he wanted to have a murti of Nityanand, whom he fondly called **Swami**, to be placed in the Gopuram building.

On hearing this, Dada informed him that he would be blessed to do this act and would go to Bombay to start the process of having Nityanand's murti made. Jananand Baba agreed to the response.

Just a simple wish was conveyed, with no specifications and no instructions regarding the size, shape, or weight by Jananand Baba. Dada came back to Bombay, wondering what he should do next.

He took his son Shri Navnit Mehta to a murti seller (one who sold idols of different gods and goddesses) who happened to have his shop opposite Papa's Stainless Steel utensils wholesale cum retail shop in the Panjrapole area.

During their discussion, Dada informed the neighbour that he wanted to have his guru's idol made from black marble since Baba had a dark complexion. But he was advised that since the murti would travel approx.1,200 Kms, from Bombay port to Mangalore port on a ship, and from there to Kanhangad by road on a truck, there was a risk of damage to the murti, causing it to become khandit (damaged), which would make the whole process and journey a waste.

Dada was then advised that he should choose the option of making the idol from **Panch Dhatu** (an alloy of five metals like gold, silver, copper, zinc, and tin). Upon further inquiry, Dada was told that there was an expert murtikar (idol maker) nearby and that he should visit him. Dada got the address of Shri Ganesh Patkar, an experienced and expert murtikar who also had his studio in South Bombay, near Dada's house.

Shri Ganesh Patkar was the murtikar who made the murtis of Nityanand Bhagwan for both Kanhangad and Guruvan temples.

Now, the challenge was determining the size, posture, and weight of the murti.

Dada informed Ganesh ji that he would provide photos of Nityanand Baba taken from every possible angle, and then Ganesh ji could decide or imagine how the murti should be made. After a few days, Dada met Ganesh ji and understood that the latter was not able to finalise the idea. Dada advised Ganesh ji to pray to Nityanand Baba and ask how he wished to be portrayed, assuring Ganesh ji that this would bring clarity.

Within a few days, Dada got a call from Ganesh ji informing him that he had received inspiration from Nityanand in his dream and that he would start the process of making the murti in **Abhay Mudra**.

A few weeks later, Ganesh ji invited Dada to come and see what he had created with Nityanand's blessings. A Mud idol looking exactly like Nityanand Baba sitting in Abhay Mudra was made.

After accepting the excellent work of art that Ganesh ji had done, Dada decided to visit Kanhangad and inform Jananand Baba about the progress of the idol. Dada visited Kanhangad and informed Jananand Baba that Swami's murti had taken shape, but it would be 6 feet tall and heavy in metal, making it impossible to place inside the Gopuram. After a short discussion, Dada asked for a solution.

Jananand Baba replied that then there should be a temple for an idol of that size. Dada informed Baba that he was willing to make an appropriately sized temple that would accommodate Swami's murti. Jananand Baba agreed to the proposal.

After Jananand Baba's affirmation, Dada returned to Bombay.

Since Ganesh ji's work was satisfactory and a perfect facial match with Nityanand Baba, the Mud idol was sent to **Indian Smelting and Refinery Ltd**. (a Birla Group company) in Bhandup East of Bombay.

Dada ordered the five metals (gold, silver, copper, zinc, and tin) in the quantities recommended by the experts at Indian Smelting. During the process of making the murti, Dada would visit the officials of Indian Smelting to see the work in progress.

On one such visit to Indian Smelting, Dada along with Ganesh Patkar, Navnitbhai, and a few other devotees were informed by the foreman that while he was in the process of making the idol and preparing the crucibles of molten metals for casting and pouring into the die mould, he heard someone saying in his ear to keep one extra crucible ready for pouring into the mould. He was surprised to hear a voice and looked around but could not see anyone. Startled and overwhelmed by this experience, he made and poured the extra crucible into the die mould.

The result was a miracle of Bhagwan and the expertise of a murtikar, which we see today in Kanhangad temple, approx. 1000 kgs in weight, six feet tall, made of Panch Dhatu, and sitting in **Abhay Mudra**. On the right side of the pedestal on which the murti is sitting, it is inscribed who made the murti, why it was made, who ordered it to be made, and when it was made. All these details were carved by Shri Ganesh Patkar, as informed by Sompuraji.

After the final touches, the murti was kept outside the workshop shed in the company's compound. It appeared that some devotees went there daily and started worshipping the murti, and from here, the process of transporting the statue from Bombay city to Kanhangad village began.

Chapter 7

The Mandir

After returning to Bombay from Kanhangad in early 1962, Dada meditated on Nityanand for his permission to initiate the plan to start the design and construction of his temple. One morning, Dada informed his family that he had a vision of his Guru Nityanand while in meditation during the night, who gave him blessings to proceed with the temple construction.

'Dada used to tell us, never to initiate a temple building activity by ourselves without direct permission from the Dev or Devi to be installed because it will not get completed, and if it does, then the Pranprathistha of the installed idol and pooja of the Kalash (the vessel placed on top of the temple) will prove fatal for the person, leading to a short life span. Only a person with adhikar (permission) can and will be able to complete the whole process and live long.

Then began another venture for Dada, to find a person who was an expert in temple architecture. Once again, there were no instructions from Jananand Baba regarding the size and model of the temple, so Dada took the initiative to find an expert in temple architecture. He knew that the Sompuras were a traditional community of master builders and craftsmen from Gujarat who built temples for many religious trusts.

So, he got in touch with Shri Prabhashankar Sompura, who lived in Ahmedabad. He had the credit of being the chief architect of the famous Shree Somnath Jyotirling Temple in Gujarat. He was also appointed as chief architect of many mandirs built by the Birla family.

Prabhashankar bhai was an authority on Vastu Shastra texts and had reinterpreted and published 20 books on classical Indian architecture. His works include hundreds of projects all over India, in a career spanning six decades. The Sompuras are a traditional community of master builders and craftsmen, originating from the Saurashtra region of Gujarat. They are natives of Prabhas Patan, also known as Somnath Patan, where their lineage extends back to ancient times. They have been and still are associated with the building activities of temples.

After a few meetings and long discussions and sharing details of the murti, Sompura ji asked Dada to visit the site where the temple had to be built and to inspect the area.

One day, Dada and Sompura ji visited Kanhangad to seek guidance from Jananand Baba on where to construct the temple. Jananand Baba informed them that Swami's temple should be on top of the rock cave hill near the Gopuram. Sompura ji and his engineers inspected the space, decided on the direction of the murti facing east, and marked the area it would take for the temple to stand tall on the hill.

Jananand Baba performed Bhumi pooja. Upon further inspection, three stones were found lying on the top of the cave hill platform near the construction site. Sompura ji asked Dada to have the stones moved before starting his work. So, Jananand Baba was approached and informed about the stones, which he then picked up and placed aside.

The temple was made only of stone, brought from Dhrangadhra, a town in Gujarat, and marble from Makrana, a city in Rajasthan. The material was transported to Mangalore port on country crafts form Dhrangadhra and from there in trucks to the temple site in Kanhangad. Most of the raw material was transported from Maharashtra, Gujarat, and Rajasthan, so Dada had to visit these towns frequently.

He would visit Kanhangad almost every month to see the progress of the temple and pay his respects to Jananand Baba. Dada asked Jananand Baba if there could be a supervisor who could oversee the whole work, inspect the raw material, and make payments to the local workers of the temple for smooth functioning. So, Shri Babana Shenoy of Nityanand Jewellery was asked by Jananand Baba to supervise the temple construction.

Swami's temple construction work was in full swing, and Sompura ji would also go to Kanhangad for inspections regularly. On the last day of Pranprathistha, Sompura ji, who was around 60 years of age at that time and had a bulky body, went up to the temple top with the support of bamboo scaffolding to take a final look at the Kalash and the Dhwaja Dand (flagpole) area of the temple. Suddenly, he lost his balance and fell from approximately 50 feet with a loud bang. Everyone present was stunned and concerned, but when one is involved in God's work, God takes care of that person. There was not a scratch on the chief architect, and he got up in one piece, bowed to God, and got back to work. ***Miracles Do Happen.***

During the temple-building process, Dada got a vision that the three stones that were put aside should be given their rightful place. Dada informed Jananand Baba, who later placed the three stones in front of Nityanand Baba's murti in a straight line, representing Akeri, Ekeri, and Bateri Baba, the Sthan Dev of the Kanhangad area. A small shrine was also made in respect of the 'Gudga deity,' who was worshipped by the nearby villagers.

The temple was completed in a record time of 9 months. Upon completion, Sompura ji informed Dada that considering the size of the temple and the cave hill on which it was standing, with the best foundation base, it would have a strong life of 500 years.

Dada regularly sent funds to support the Bal Bhojan in Kanhangad, Guruvan, and Kumbal ashrams.

When Nityanand Baba's murti arrived in Kanhangad in 1963, it was painted in a greyish-blue oil paint as Nityanand Baba's skin complexion was dark. Over the years, the murti was painted a few more times, which created a thick coat of oil paint, dulling the features of the idol. In 1989-90, Dadi (Vimlaben) and I visited Kanhangad to attend the Dhwaja changing ceremony on Pranprathistha Day. There was a devotee who had accompanied one of the trustees, who was an expert in restoring murtis. He came to Dadi and suggested that if the paint was removed from the statue and it was restored to the original look of Panch Dhatu (an alloy of five metals), it would look more beautiful, and Baba's features would show.

He informed Dadi that if she permitted him to carry out the process, there would be more feelings of positive vibration coming from the murti. He suggested the necessary process of transferring Pran from the original murti to the small idol of Nityanand Baba had to be done. For that, a priest was called to perform the pooja for transferring Pran and to restore the same back to the original murti afterward. After Dadi gave her affirmation, and the Pran transferring pooja was done, the expert then shut the doors of the Garbhagriha, removed the colour from the murti, and the process took two days. On the third day, a translucent chemical was applied to the murti, and he assured everyone that as time passed, the murti would shine and glow to its original divinity.

What we see today is the original Murti.

Chapter 8

Transporting the Murti to Kanhangad

Dada booked space to load the precious cargo with Scindia Steam Navigation Shipping Co. for transporting from Bombay Port to Mangalore Port. The murti was onboard Saraswathi steamer (passenger ship) for its sea journey to Mangalore port. The PanchDhatu murti was packed in an empty wooden box and placed on the deck of the ship. Some devotees decided to travel with Bhagwan on the ship until the final destination. The journey took two days, and during the sail, the devotees sat in front of the box, chanting mantras and singing bhajans. Upon reaching Mangalore, the box was loaded onto a truck, and the devotees also boarded the same. As the news spread that Bhagwan's murti was travelling by road to Kanhangad, those who knew the divinity of Bhagwan also joined the caravan of their own free will.

The road journey from Mangalore to Kanhangad was slow and steady as the roads were narrow, and there were many followers on the journey. The caravan reached Kanhangad ashram. The wooden box was unloaded and opened inside the ashram. The devotees witnessed a miracle—there were fresh flowers and fruits at the feet of the murti, which were not put there at the time of sealing the box, as they would have become stale after almost three days of sea and road journey. His divine presence and acceptance were witnessed by many. After the box with the statue in it was opened, it was taken for a road show in Kanhangad village and then returned to the ashram in the evening.

Babubhai (Dada) had planned to take his family, his mother, the extended family of his brothers, and some devotees, totalling approximately 100 persons, to Kanhangad by railway and had booked two tourist coaches with attached kitchen from the Indian Railways a few months in advance to travel to Kanhangad and also to return back to Bombay.

It would take three days to reach Kanhangad because there were no direct trains. So, the train, Madras Mail would go to Arakkonam from Bombay's VT (Victoria Terminus) station, and then after a few hours of layover, the bogies would be reattached to another coal steam engine of Madras Mangalore Express which would take them to a small station in Kanhangad village. In those days, it was a medium gauge, single-track rail route.

Chapter 9

Kanhangad Mandir Pranprathistha - 29th April 1963 – Vaishakh, Shashti, Shukla Paksh

It was a time of huge gatherings in Kanhangad, there was a mood of festivity for many days. The temple was completed and awaiting the murti to be installed and the Pranprathistha to be done.

Dada and his family arrived in Kanhangad in the summer of April 1963. Dada and his immediate family stayed in a room near Jananand Baba's room which was made comfortable for a few days as electricity was not continuously available. The rest of the devotees and visitors were given accommodation in Shri Durga School near the bus stand. Dada also took four cooks with him to prepare Gujarati food to their taste, as the South Indian food was not preferred by all from Bombay.

As per the local newspaper of Kanhangad, there were an estimated few lakhs visitor (a few hundred thousand) in Kanhangad.

31

It was said that hundreds of visitors slept on the railway tracks, as there were very few trains passing at night from Kanhangad in those days.

To perform the Pranprathistha Vidhi, expert pujaris were called from Gokarna, a town in Karnataka state. Jananand Baba had sent a Brahmin from Gokarna to meet Dada in Mumbai and explain to him the whole process of consecration. But there was a small problem—Dada did not know any South Indian languages, and the Brahmin could not speak Hindi. So, Dada took the support of an acquaintance who owned an Udupi restaurant to translate the conversation.

Dada was informed about how many Brahmins would be present and what would be required in the grand pooja/yagna. The Brahmin informed Dada that they would arrange and bring all the necessary items required.

The pujaris from Gokarna were the best at conducting the Pranprathistha (consecration) Vidhi. Dada and Dadi sat in this Vidhi (process). The installation of the murti was done, and then the actual Prana was infused (divine cosmic energy was invoked) into the murti to bring it to life by the pujaris, which was done at the stroke of midnight.

First, nine precious stones with some gold and silver were placed at the base of the murti. Then, Bhagwan's murti was installed inside the Garbhagriha of the temple under Sompura ji's supervision, who was also present at the time to assist in the process. All the Vedic mantra chants were sung by the pujaris, then the gold-plated metal Kalash was consecrated and lifted to the top of the temple Shikhar (top) and fixed around the stone Kalash. Then, the Dhwaja Dand, which was also gold and silver-plated, along with the Dhwaja (the flag size was made according to the vidhi of temple-making), was also taken up to be installed in its place.

The consecration process was completed with the blessing of the divine. Bhagwan's Padukas were also installed in the temple right in front of the murti, above the three stones of the Sthan dev, which was made from pure pink marble.

After three days and nights, the vidhi (process) was complete. Nityanand Bhagwan's murti was installed, and at midnight, the Pranprathistha was done in the Garbhagriha!

In the early morning, Dada (Grandfather) and Dadi (Grandmother), with their family, went to meet Jananand Baba to take his blessings. Baba was very happy and pleased with the devotion and dedication shown by Dada, and he blessed Dada and his family by giving him a silver thali (plate) with some flowers and fruits along with a Krishna murti carved out of wood, as a gift.

Jananand Baba was so pleased that he asked Dada to take the keys to the ashram, stay there, and take care of the day-to-day activities of the ashram. **Dada, with folded hands, said that he was a Sansari (householder) and not a Sanyasi and very respectfully declined Baba's offer.**

Jananand Baba informed Dada that his deed was so great that it had purified the path of the 72 generations that came before him and also of those who would come after him.

The evening of the third and final day of the Pranprathistha ceremony was attended by many government officials, journalists, and by Maharashtra's Chief Minister Shri M. Kanamvar and Kerala

Chief Minister Shri R. Shankar, who were invited as chief guests. They felicitated Shri Babubhai H. Mehta (Lokhandwala) for his achievement in the presence of Shri Jananand Baba and other devotees. Dada gave Shri Jananand Baba Rs. 5,000/- to start the Nityanand Polytechnic College in Kanhangad so that the youth would study and prosper in their lives.

It was reported in the local newspapers/magazines that there were an estimated 5 lakh (five hundred thousand) people who attended the grand function, and everyone was served food with the blessings of Maa Annapurna Devi (Goddess of Food & Prosperity). The food was sufficient for all three days of the festivity.

After getting blessings and permission from Jananand Baba, Dada, and his family returned home to Bombay. On the next day of reaching Bombay, Dada got a trunk call from the Kanhangad ashram and was informed that the pink marble paduka (two-foot impressions) which was kept in front of Bhagwan's murti over Akeri, Ekeri, and Bateri Baba had developed a black mark on the right foot and a little black mark on the left foot on the very next day of the Pranprathishtha day, on its own.

It seemed like Bhagwan had accepted Dada's Bhav bhakti and Shram bhakti by showing his omnipresence.

Chapter 10

Ram became Nityanand

Nityanand Baba was said to be a Swayambhu !!

In Kerala, during the time of the British Raj, there lived a poor agricultural couple named Chathur Nair and Uniamma in the small village of Thuneri, Calicut. One stormy night, Uniamma had a vision of Lord Vishnu and Shiva, telling her to visit a nearby temple early in the morning. Following their instructions, she set out before dawn, despite the rain. To her surprise, she found a baby boy under a tree, sheltered by a large cobra spreading its hood over him.

Worried about his wife being gone too long, Chathur Nair asked their employer, Ishwar Iyer, to accompany him to find her. When they arrived, they saw the baby surrounded by snakes. The snakes circled the child three times and then disappeared into the ground. Ishwar Iyer asked Uniamma to take the baby home, which she happily did.

When the baby turned one, Ishwar and a friend named him *Ram*, meaning 'the one who brings bliss'. The naming ceremony was held at the Shri Ayyappa temple. Chathur was very fond of Ram, and before he passed away, he told Uniamma to take special care of him. With her own children to look after, Uniamma requested Ishwar Iyer to care for Ram as one of his own. Ishwar agreed and treated Ram like his own son.

One day, Ram fell seriously ill, and no medicines seemed to help. In desperation, Uniamma visited temples, praying for his recovery. Early one morning, she was stopped by a tall man carrying a crow. He instructed her to kill the crow, collect its blood, and rub it on the boy's body. She was also told to cook the meat in ghee and feed Ram a spoonful each day. She followed his instructions, and Ram soon recovered, but his skin turned dark and remained so until his *samadhi*.

Ram was a bright, healthy, and much-loved child. When he was six, Uniamma passed away, and Ishwar took full responsibility for him. As a devout Brahmin and lawyer, Ishwar would read the Ramayana, Bhagavad Gita and Mahabharata to Ram, who listened intently. Ram's presence brought Ishwar a sense of divine peace. Ishwar even took Ram to his work, and to his surprise, Ram could predict the outcome of court cases before they were even heard.

A passing Brahmin astrologer identified Ram as an incarnation of Shiva, which further strengthened Ishwar's bond with the boy. Though Ishwar tried to send Ram to school, Ram refused, insisting that he already had the wisdom he needed.

As Ram grew older, Ishwar took him on pilgrimages to places like Kashi, Varanasi, and Triveni Sangam. Before returning home,

Ram expressed his desire to visit the Himalayas for deep meditation. Over time, Ishwar distributed his property among his children, giving Ram an equal share, but Ram refused it, saying the world was already his and material possessions held no meaning for him.

One Sunday morning, as Ishwar offered water to the Sun god, he shared his wish with Ram to see Surya Narayan in his true form. Shortly after, Ishwar had a vision of the Sun god, and in a state of bliss, he exclaimed, **"Ram, you have given me divine happiness. You are my Nityanand, and you will be Nityanand to all."** Ishwar then passed away peacefully, having attained the supreme state of *Sat Chit Anand.*

From that moment, 'Ram became to be known as Nityanand'.

Nityanand performed the last rites for Ishwar and travelled to Kashi to immerse his ashes in the Ganga. He spent time in the holy city, wearing saffron robes and living on fruits and milk. After a period of meditation in various temples, he wandered across India, visiting countries like Burma, and Sri Lanka, and his presence was felt even in countries as far as the UK and USA. Many devotees claim to have seen him before and after his samadhi.

When Nityanand returned to Koyilandy, people didn't recognise him, as he had grown from the boy, they once knew who had now become an *Avdhoot. In Sanatan Dharma, an Avdhoot is a spiritually enlightened being who has detached from the world's illusions.*

Nityanand travelled through South India, performing miracles and helping the poor. Children adored him, as he would magically produce sweets for them from nowhere.

Chapter 11

Play of Divinity in Kanhangad

Till 1862, Kanhangad was in Bekal Taluk under the Bombay Presidency. On April 15, 1862, when the Dakshina Kannada region became part of the Madras Presidency, it was included in the Kasaragod taluka. After the formation of Kerala state, Kasaragod taluk (district) was divided and Kanhangad came under Hosdurg taluka on 1 January 1957.

People of Kanhangad saw a lean dark swami who had only put on a loin cloth, cleaning the vegetation within the old fort area and tilting the ground. They were surprised to find that the swami had employed many workers to help level the ground in the fort.

Swami had begun working on the reddish rock hill. Under Swamiji's direction and planning, the labourers dug into the hill. This news spread all over the small town. It was a miracle that he paid the workers their daily wages by pulling out money from his loin cloth. The villagers came regularly to see this magic of Nityanand and he began to be called Kala Sadhu.

This news reached the government officials of the area and there was a rumour that the swami was into suspicious activity and that he started encroaching on government land.

The government officials came to see what the Swamiji was doing. They asked him where he was getting the cash to pay the workers their daily wages. Swamiji jumped in the big pond nearby and after some time came up with a fresh dry bundle of currency notes and showed it to the officials. That was an unbelievable sight as there was a big crocodile in that pond. After showing them the money Swami threw that bundle into the pond and said, 'The crocodile has the money, go and take it if you want'.

The police then reported the matter to the District Collector of Tirunelveli, E M Gawne, I.C.S. The British formed this district in 1790 and located it in the southern parts of Tamilnadu, including Virudhunagar district, areas of Western Ghats, Tenkasi district, Kanyakumari district, and Tuticorin district. E. M. Gawne was a district collector for a few months in 1923.

The District Collector agreed to go and see the work as the whole inquiry was reported to his office. He came with the police chiefs and other important people on horses, along with his dog.

Swamiji was sitting inside a cave. When they reached the rocky hill, the Collector's dog picked up a scent and ran towards the cave. The Collector came in, leaving the other officers outside. He took off his shoes, entered the sacred cave, and bowed to Swami, who greeted him with a smile. The Collector asked Swamiji, "Who are you making this for?" Swamiji replied, "Not for this one. Do you want it? Take it." It's unclear what exactly happened, but the

Collector left the cave and told his staff not to disturb Swami and let him continue his work.

On his way back to his guest house in Hosdurg, he saw something, a miracle. The road he had come from was named after him, 'E.M. Gawne Road'. There was a name board at the start of the road that was not there before. It was a message to the collector and his team that the Swami was divine and enlightened.

Within a few years, a rough design of 48 caves was made inside the rock hill. Swamiji did not take any help from any architect as it was his design and shaped by his own hands, inside out.

Nityanand Bhagwan performed many miracles while in Kanhangad and travelling through Kerala, Karnataka, the Malabar coast, and then to Maharashtra. **He eventually settled in Ganeshpuri.**

Nityanand Baba lived in Kanhangad and Guruvan. At an early age, he did tapasya in Guruvan and from there he went and stayed in Kanhangad and did the basic designing and primary work of the caves, all by himself and with the employed worker.

Because of his divine *leelas* (miracles) in Maharashtra and southern parts of India, people knew who Nityanand was.

Chapter 12

Guruvan Temple – Pranprathistha - April 1965 – Vaisakha, Ashtami, Shukla Paksh

Guruvan mandir was completed in 1965, two years after Kanhangad mandir.

During his teenage years, Nityanand Baba spent many years in Guruvan, where he lived in natural caves. He did miracles for the good of his devotees.

In 1961, Jananand Baba purchased Guruvan from the Raja of Nileshwar for Rs. 5,000, using his savings. He wanted to keep the holy place because his Guru had meditated there and shown many miracles. Guruvan means guru's forest. It was a dense forest with wild animals, birds, snakes, and insects. Beautiful hills covered in forest are on three sides, with just one way in and out.

Jananand Baba used to say that saints and divine beings are sitting inside the caves in invisible form and when the time is right, they will emerge to uphold the Sanatan Dharma. To protect the sanctity of the caves, Jananand Baba had the cave sealed off. He did not want anyone to enter the divine space. Jananand Baba never allows anyone to stay overnight in Guruvan. Many who did not listen to Baba had supernatural/paranormal experiences and never dared to return to that place. Only with Jananand Baba's permission could one stay in Guruvan without experiencing any unimaginable and unforgettable experience.

The Sthan Dev of Guruvan, Shri Malahvir Raja was a very strict deity.

Dada with Nityanand's permission and Jananand Baba's blessings completed another temple in Guruvan, where Bhagwan at a young age had done tapasya and stayed there before coming to Kanhangad and designed and constructed the Gufas (caves).

Shri Prabhasankar Sompura was again appointed as the architect of the temple and it was also made of stone and marble brought from Gujarat and Rajasthan states. This temple was also built like the temples in north India, unlike South Indian temples.

It was a big job for the workers to do their daily tasks. The materials arrived at Mangalore port, then travelled by road to Kanhangad through Nileshwar village, and finally to Guruvan by road as well.

Once the temple material reached the outskirts of the Guruvan area it had to be taken to the riverbank. After crossing the river in small boats, the workers would carry the materials on their heads and walk up the hill through the forest to the temple site. It was literally an uphill task and with Bhagwan Nityanand's blessings, the temple was completed.

Nityanand's murti was also taken to the Guruvan temple premises similarly. It is believed that an elephant was hired to transport the murti to the temple.

On Jananand Baba's wish, Dada also built a small shrine of Shri Malahvir swami, where two real-time swords of the Sthan Dev of Guruvan area, were installed for worship. Near the Sthan dev, there were eight stones shaped like shivling, in a circular form. Jananand Baba informed that they were Aastha Siddhis (eight virtues) which have been there for a very long time. Many divine beings come to Guruvan, in both visible and invisible forms, to meditate and gain more power and wisdom. It is believed that Guruvan is a possible location where beings from other dimensions/realms would come and go.

There are caves inside the mountains adjoining the temple and it was said that Nityanand had done his tapasya and also many saints and sages had done the same before him. There was just one freshwater well near the caves. Nityanand wanted fresh running water for daily use, so he got water from the mountain and named it Papnashini Ganga. This stream of water flowed from inside the mountain and then passed underground the temple and came out from the Gaumukh (cow's mouth) which was made with the temple. Anyone can drink the water and have a bath with top-quality water, helping to solve body problems inside and out.

There was only one path to go in and back as the site was surrounded by forest on three sides. Because of the difficult path, this mandir took a little longer to build compared to the size and logistical ease of the Kanhangad temple location.

The soil in the forest was very fertile and many different fruits, nuts, spices, and coconuts grew there.

Dada took Ba and his children to Guruvan again to perform the Pranprathistha ceremony. He placed the Murti of Bhagwan as a young man, made from the same five metals - Panch Dhatu, which was also made by the Indian Smelting Company in Bombay.

Shri Ganesh Patkar was the Murtikar of the Guruvan temple's Murti too.

This Murti was in Padmasan pose and had a younger look of a tapasvi as Nityanand had stayed there in his youth and became one with divine energy.

This occasion was attended by Lt. Governor of Pondicherry Shir Thiru S. L. Silam and other thousands of devotees.

After the Pranprathistha Vidhi was completed Babubhai, Vimlaben, and their three children went to meet Jananand Baba. **'Jananand Baba gave his blessings to Dada, Dadi, and his family and informed Dada that Swami (Nityanand Baba) had mentioned to him that one day a Raja (king) would come and build temples in Kanhangad and Guruvan'.**

Dada bowed to Jananand Baba with the highest gratitude and travelled back to Bombay.

After 44 years, in 2009, 'Swami Nityanand Ashram Public Trust' decided to demolish the Guruvan temple. The Murti from this temple is now in Jananand Baba's room at the Kanhangad ashram, for darshan. A new temple was built in the South Indian style, and Pranprathistha happened on 6th May 2011, on Akshaya Tritiya tithi.

Jananand Baba had permitted different Bhatjis (pujaris) to stay in Guruvan and do daily pooja/aarti in the temple. In 1975 Jananand Baba allowed Swami Vidyanand to stay in Kanhangad ashram. After a few years, he was told to go to Guruvan and stay there. He has been giving his seva and doing pooja/aarti in the temple since 2004.

Every year our family has maintained the tradition of offering Dhwaja to this new temple also.

Chapter 13

Story of Sadguru Jananand Swami

Jananand Baba was born in 1893 in Hejmadi, a village close to Mulki in South Karnataka. As a kid, he was strong and healthy, and he loved playing football with his friends. One day, while playing, the ball rolled onto the road. When he went to get it, he met a man who looked very important. It was Shri Nityanand Bhagwan in his Avdhoot form. He blessed young Baba, and it was their first meeting. They both felt something special between them.

Baba had a strong desire to find spiritual truth. He went to Bombay and got a job in a restaurant. There, he quickly learned to cook a variety of dishes, both sweet and savoury. While working, he would get lost in deep meditation, thinking of God. On many occasions, the food he was cooking would catch fire while he was meditating.

One day, when the food caught fire again, Baba reached into the boiling oil with his bare hands to take it out. His hands were not badly hurt, just a few small burns, which healed quickly after he applied honey. The restaurant owner became worried and thought something was wrong with Baba, maybe an evil spirit. In those days, people often believed in such things. The owner took Baba to meet Shri Balakrishna Maharaj, a well-known healer. When Balakrishna Maharaj met Baba, he realised immediately, there was something special about Baba. He told the owner that Baba had the power of a great yogi, and in time, this would become clear.

Balakrishna Maharaj suggested Baba to visit Gangaapur, where the sacred *Padukas* of Shri Narasimha Maharaj are kept.

In Gangapur, he meditated at the rivers' bank. Over time, many people started coming to him because of his spiritual presence. It is said that Lord Dattatray appeared before Baba, pleased with his dedication.

After this, Baba went to Kanhangad, where he met Shri Nityanand Bhagwan again. Nityanand was digging caves out of a large rock with his hands. Baba, who was strong, helped him. Nityanand affectionately called him Maruti, another name for Hanuman, and said Baba's crowbar was like Hanuman's Gadha (club), showing how much, he admired Baba's dedication.

In 1938, Nityanand told Baba to go on a pilgrimage to the Himalayas. Baba set off barefoot, carrying only a trident to help him walk through the snow. His journey was tough, but Baba said he overcame all the challenges with the help of his guru, Nityanand.

During his travels in the Himalayas, Baba came across many Tibetan tribes. One day, he met a tribal leader who became angry with Baba for entering his land. Baba was cold and tired and politely asked for some tea. The chief ordered his men to pour boiling tea over Baba and let their dogs loose at him. Before leaving, Baba predicted that Tibet would face hardship in the near future, and years later, the Chinese invasion of Tibet forced the Lamas and local tribes to run away from their own lands.

Baba was in the Himalayas for many years, visiting holy places like Rishikesh, Badrinath, Kedarnath, Kailash and Mansarovar. The journey was hard, but he kept going, following the spiritual path his guru had given him.

Bhagwan had made Swami Jananand perform a Yagna - Anuasthan (mahapooja) at Gangaapur in Maharashtra. After a long journey, Baba came back to Ganeshpuri. When Baba arrived, Bhagwan sent his *sevaks* to bring him. On seeing Baba Nityanand, he was filled with joy and he embraced him.

Baba had grown tired from his travels and had a long beard and knotted hair. His body was cold from the journey, so he immediately jumped into the hot spring known as *Surya Kund* and entered into a deep meditative state. The water was so hot it could cook rice, but Baba was not harmed.

In Ganeshpuri, Bhagwan had moved to the new Kailash building and stayed there. His old room was kept locked for Bhagwan only. When Jananand Swami came to Ganeshpuri, he was asked by Bhagwan to stay in that room which was a big honour for him.

Nityanand then gave Baba the name *Jananand*, which means 'one who is a joy to others'.

Then after a couple of days, Baba was asked by Bhagwan to look after Kanhangad Ashram and finish the work on the caves that Bhagwan had begun. So, Baba moved to Kanhangad and lived there for the rest of his life. Baba took on this duty with full dedication. He worked hard to turn the once-wild area into a peaceful and well-organised place. Ashram became an integral part of the Kanhangad township.

The ashram was built and maintained by Jananand Baba since 1925. There were two rooms, a long corridor with a very large empty area of the ashram compound. It was adjoining the railway tracks. There were two freshwater wells for the daily chorus. Electricity was a luxury. There were also two freshwater ponds near the cow shelter which was filled with fishes. There was a kitchen and a few helpers who supported Jananand Baba in day-to-day activities. Shri Krishna Nayyar personally gave seva to Jananand Baba and stayed in the adjoining room and took care of Baba's daily needs. Meenakshi Amma who was a household devotee also gave seva in the ashram who took care of the food preparation and maintenance of the ashram along with her other colleagues. The children of these workers also gave their service to Jananand Baba and worked for the ashram.

Jananand Baba put in great efforts to grow herbs, coconuts, Spices, and nuts in 49 acres of land at Guruvan and large farm of Kanhangad ashram. All the produce was sold in the wholesale market which gave a reasonable annual income and that income was used to maintain the ashram, and school and pay wages to the workers. With Baba's leadership, the ashram flourished, supported by donations from followers all over the world.

Jananand Baba made sure that the ashram provided free food and accommodation to everyone who came, no matter their background. One of the most important traditions at the ashram was *Bal Bhojan*, where free meals were provided to children every day. This tradition continues to this day.

Chapter 14

Temple of Param Pujya Swami Jananand Baba

Swami Jananand Baba's Samadhi temple was built on the ground level near the Cave Rock hill in the ashram at Kanhangad. The Samadhi temple was completed & "Pranprathishtha Puja " of the murti was performed in the presence of Swami Sadanand Baba (Padiyar Swami) who lived in the Kushalnagar area, on 8th of December 1989. The Murti was made of "Panch Dhatu" and was designed and made in Khar, a suburb of Mumbai, by a famous sculptor, Mr. Sonavadekar.

Among the monks who worshipped Bhagwan Nityanand, there were three who stood out for their deep spiritual achievements and total devotion to Bhagwan.

- **Tulsi Amma** was called **'Vairagya Murti,'** meaning someone free from worldly desires. Baba blessed her to write the Chidakasha Gita.

- **Shaligram Swami**, known as **'Agni Devata'** or the Fire God, whose samadhi temple is in Ganeshpuri, close to the Bhagwan's samadhi temple.

- **Jananand Baba was known to be a manifestation of the 'Dattatray Avatar'**, whose samadhi temple is in Kanhangad ashram.

Sadanand Baba (Padiyar swami) was asked by Nityanand Baba to go from Ganeshpuri to Kanhangad and stay there forever and inform the devotees about Nitya tatva (Nityanand) and offer his services to the devotees and continue doing that only.

When Sadanand Swami met Jananand Baba, he was asked to stay in the Kushalnagar area. So, he stayed there for over 40 years until he passed away.

Jananand Baba took care of the Ashram and his Master's temple and never tried to promote himself. For everything, he put Bhagwan as the cause and worked like a true 'Karma Yogi'.

Bhagwan's love for both Kanhangad Ashram and Swami Jananand was quite evident in his desire to meet Jananand and visit Kanhangad during his last days. He asked Shri Devraya Pai and Shri Laxmansha Khoday to make arrangements to take him to Kanhangad. Unfortunately, none of the devotees could complete this wish. On the night of 7th August 1961, just one day before he took Mahasamadhi, he constantly remembered Swami Jananand and repeatedly asked whether he had come. When Bhagwan was told he had still not been able to reach Ganeshpuri, Bhagwan was sad. Jananand Baba could reach only on the 9th of August and not before Bhagwan attained Mahasamadhi on the 8th of August 1961 at 10.43 am.

On another occasion, during Dada's visit to Kanhangad for the annual Pranprathistha ceremony, Jananand Baba announced that he would take samadhi very soon.

All the devotees present there in the ashram become sad. They knew Baba liked Lokhanwalaseth a lot, so they asked Dada to talk to Baba about delaying his decision. Dada then asked Krishna Nayyar to arrange a meeting with Baba. After getting Baba's permission, Dada met him in his room at the ashram and spoke to him alone. No one knows what they talked about.

Dada told everyone that it was a divine order for Baba to take Samadhi. He also said he asked Baba to choose the date of 'Datta Jayanti' for this, and Baba agreed.

Dada and other devotees suggested Baba to form a trust that would look after the functioning of the Kanhangad ashram, Guruvan area, college, school, and other properties of the ashram. On hearing this Baba said **"To dus aadmi aur gyaara dimag kam kare ga"** (so there will be 10 people and 11 brains at work), Baba understood what was needed at that time and agreed to the idea.

A trust was formed with some very close followers, and Dada was one of the founding members.

Chapter 15

Tulabhar

On **10th April 1982**, Dada decided to show his highest respect and admiration for Jananand Baba before he took Mahasamadhi, so it was decided to organise a Tulabhar ceremony (an ancient Hindu practice in which a person is weighed against a commodity). The event involved using a 1/- Rupee coin for weighing Baba. A total of 60 kg of these coins were collected from banks in Bombay, Mangalore and Kanhangad by Dada for the occasion. Baba sat on one side, and on the other side, there was a big basket for the coins. Dada's family and other devotees took turns putting bowls of coins into the basket. After a while, the basket became heavy, and Jananand Baba's feet lifted off the ground.

About 55 kg of coins lifted Baba's feet off the ground. Thousands of believers and local people from nearby villages came to witness this holy event and enjoyed Prasad in the afternoon and evening.

The coins were given to the devotees as Prasad. After the Tulabhar was done, Dada took us to receive blessings from Jananand Baba.

Baba placed his hand on our heads, and we felt extremely lucky to be blessed by the Paramapoojya Swami Jananand Baba.

Final Darshan of his Guru

In October 1982, a couple of months before taking Samadhi, Jananand Baba visited Ganeshpuri & performed puja of his Swami (his Guru) in the Samadhi temple of his beloved Sadhguru Nityanand Bhagwan.

A grand welcome was done by Baba's devotees on his arrival at the Bombay airport and also in Ganeshpuri. Baba stayed on the ground floor of Banglorewala's building in Ganeshpuri for a few days, where he gave darshan, every day, to thousands of devotees of Nityanand Bhagwan & of his own, who had come to seek his blessings. Many of the devotees of Nityanand Bhagwan from the monk order were also present there to take blessings from Baba. During Jananand Baba's visit to Ganeshpuri, Baba took a bath in the hot water springs and paid his respects to Bhagwan at his samadhi.

Inside the Samadhi temple, the first Aarti was done for Bhagwan's murti on the Samadhi. Then, the same Aarti was waved before Swami Jananand Baba, which is a very rare honour. Jananand Baba was sitting opposite Nityanand's Samadhi, outside the Garbhagriha. The poojari went to Baba and performed his Aarti and immediately Baba went into a trance, his eyes open and rolled upwards, not blinking until the Aarti was finished.

To this day, no person in monk order has been offered Aarti in front of Bhagwan and more so with the same Aarti which has been first shown to Bhagwan. This was Bhagwan's way of acknowledging

Jananand Baba's love, sacrifice, hard work, dedication, and devotion to Bhagwan Nityanand.

This was the last visit of Baba to Ganeshpuri before his Samadhi in Kanhangad.

Swami Jananand Baba attained his Mahasamadhi on 27th December 1982.

Long before taking samadhi, Jananand Baba had appointed a pujari to perform the daily aartis of swami Nityanand in his temple. A few days after the Pranprathistha of Jananand Baba's temple, that pujari got a vision of Jananand Baba asking him to perform Shiv's puja for Nityanand and Vishnu's pooja at his samadhi. It was therefore inferred that Nityanand Baba was Shiv tattva and Jananand Baba was Vishnu tattva.

Jananand Baba's temple was built by **'Swami Nityanand Ashram Public Trust'** and it was planned and constructed by a relative of the late Shri Prabhasankar Sompura, Shri Hargovindbhai Sompura. Baba's murti was made of Panch Dhatu by a well-known Murtikar Shri Sonavadekar in Khar, a suburb of Bombay. Many devotees contributed precious metal and cash for the making of this murti.

We, as Dada's family, were fortunate to be part of the Bhumi pooja and also to place a few of the 8 stones of the Vaastu Purush in different directions. There were other devotees who were also fortunate enough to be part of the ceremony.

Pranprathsitha of Jananand Baba's temple was done on 8th December 1989.

Every time Dada visited Kanhangad, Baba would come to meet Dada in room no. 8 every morning, which Baba would allot to Dada and ask him to stay in that room whenever he visited Kanhangad. This room was one of the room clusters near the freshwater well.

Baba would come to check on our comfort and inquired if we had tea and breakfast. He would sit on the patio outside the room with Dada for some time and get back to his normal routine in the ashram. Then before the afternoon aarti of Nityanand Bhagwan, we would get the opportunity to sit near Jananand Baba's feet, sometimes in the ashram hall's entrance, opposite the trust office, or near the big Pipal tree in the compound.

That time was unique. **In 1982,** Baba shared that in a person's horoscope, the planet Shani (Saturn) stays for seven & half years and this happens every 30 years. Majority of people experience this cycle of planet Shani only two times in their lifetime and then they pass away before the third cycle comes. **Baba told Dada, "Seth, your seat is ready up there, and there are three seats in total. One of them is yours."** This meant that the seats for Nityanand, Jananand, and Dada were in the higher realm. Baba also told Dada that his time was coming soon and he should prepare to leave his body and join the divine.

On 21ˢᵗ December 1986, Dada's soul left this world to become one with his Guru in the higher realm.

For him, his 'Sadguru Bhagwan Shri Nityanand Baba'.

Then Jananand Baba said that since he was in a human body, planet Shani's cycle was affecting him too, and this was why he was not feeling well. On inquiring about his swollen feet by Dada which made it difficult for him to walk, he informed Dada that for many years visitors came and bowed down at his feet and wished for different things including the improvement of their health or the health of their loved ones, therefore he had to take their pain and that was the reason his feet are swollen, **"Sab aata hai aur idhar dalke jata hai"** (everyone comes and put it at my feet). Baba also mentioned that he was experiencing the third seven-and-a-half-year cycle of the Shani planet and very few people in the world would survive this and that it was the last Shani cycle for him (Baba).

At that moment, he also said something very important and surprising, 'Lokhandwala Seth, **"Mere aur Swami mai aaj koi farak nahi hai, hum dono ek hai"** (right now, there is no difference between Swami and me; we are both equal) and my samadhi temple will also be built in the ashram grounds'.

What a great transformation !! "Man becomes God."

Chapter 16

Ganeshpuri Mandir

Nityanand Baba took Mahasamadhi on 8th August 1961.

Pranprathistha of the Samadhi temple was done on 8th February 1973 and it was 'Vasant Panchami day'.

Dada was one of the founder trustees of Ganeshpuri Trust. He was appointed as Treasurer for the trust. Dada also looked after the arrangements for the Bal Bhojan meals. After Dada had completed the two temples of Nityanand Bhagwan, Shri Bhausaheb Vartak who was the Chairperson of the trust and also a cabinet minister in the Maharashtra state government, came to see him. Shri Vartak was also a follower of Bhagwan and had a good relationship with Dada.

He informed Dada that after Baba's samadhi, the trust had tried to do Bhumi Pooja to enable the construction of the Samadhi temple, but every time they tried, they were unable to complete the process for some strange reasons. It had been many years since Nityanand

Baba took samadhi. Bhausaheb ji requested Dada to assist them in building the temple because he had successfully consecrated and completed two temples in Kanhangad and Guruvan in Kerala within 4 years (1963 & 1965 respectively) of Baba's Mahasamadhi.

Dada informed Bhausaheb that he did not have any instruction from Nityanand or Jananand Baba to initiate the process by himself, so, he will pray to Nityanand for his guidance. After a few days, Dada informed Bhausaheb that they should go ahead with the Bhoomi puja and then proceed with the temple construction. The trustees unanimously decided that Shri Babubhai Hargovindas Mehta (Lokhandwala) and his wife Smt. Vimlaben Babubhai Mehta would do the Bhumi Pooja and the trust would take care of the end-to-end process of the temple construction in Ganeshpuri.

On 9th August 1968, Bhumi Poojan was done with Nityanand Bhagwan's wish by Dada (grandfather) & Dadi (grandmother) and then the Samadhi temple came into reality.

Once the bhumi pooja was completed the temple building work was given to Prabhashankar Sompura ji, the architect of the Kanhangad and Guruvan temples. Samadhi temple process started and today we have a grand temple over Nityanand Baba's samadhi with a sitting area of 3,000 sq. feet without any pillars supporting the roof to facilitate the devotees to have an unobstructed view of Bhagwan's murti and samadhi. Large donations poured in from thousands of devotees for the temple construction and for making of the Murti.

A Panch Dhatu murti in a sitting posture was installed in the mandir in Ganeshpuri which was made by a famous murtikar Shri Wagh who had his studio opposite Bombay Chowpatty.

One can find the names of all the Founder Trustees inscribed on a big marble tablet cemented on the wall inside the temple on the right-hand side of the samadhi murti.

Ganeshpuri is a small village which is approx. 90 km from Mumbai and 2 km from Shree Vajeshwari temple.

Chapter 17

Legacy and Continuation

The spiritual journey and temple-building efforts initiated by Dada left a profound impact on our family.

The legacy of devotion, faith, and service has been passed down to us, influencing the lives and values of 3 generations after him.

Babubhai's children and we the grandchildren grew up witnessing the deep faith and dedication he had towards Swami Nityanand and the temples he built. This spiritual environment shaped our upbringing, instilling the importance of preserving and continuing this legacy.

The temples stand as a testament of our family's commitment to the spiritual roots, and values imparted by Dada, which continue to guide our lives.

The importance of preserving this legacy is deeply felt by our family, who see it as our duty to honour and maintain the spiritual and cultural heritage passed down to us.

We regularly visit the temples, especially during important religious occasions, and that has become a cherished tradition within the family.

Personal anecdotes highlight the continued devotion of our family to the temples. For instance, every year, we have maintained the tradition of offering the Dhwaja (flag) to the new temple in Guruvan, demonstrating our ongoing commitment to honouring Swami Nityanand and preserving the sacred spaces he once blessed.

Chapter 18

Gratitude

Dada did not inscribe his name on both the temples even though he had funded the end-to-end process of the temples' building and the murti making from his successful business.

Dada had informed my grandmother and my father as he was the eldest son, that he had given all the rights and responsibilities of Kanhangad and Guruvan temples to Jananand Baba after the Pranprathistha ceremonies. So, he, his family, and the future generation should not worry about the maintenance of the temples. He also said that there was no compulsion on his coming generation to give seva to the temples in the future.

Dada said, "Nityanand nu Nityanand ne Aapyu. Nityanand Arpan" (it belonged to Nityanand so given to Nityanand) "If you can do the annual Pranparthistha ceremony then do it with humbleness, devotion, and faith, if you cannot for whatever reasons in the future do not worry, take it as a Will of Bhagwan (GOD)".

With the blessings of Nityanand Bhagwan and Jananand Baba, our family has either sent the Dhwaja or reached Kanhangad and Guruvan with the Dhwaja on the annual Pranprathistha day for the last 61 years.

As we conclude this journey of faith and devotion, we express our deep gratitude to Nityanand Baba for his divine presence and his blessings. We also acknowledge the support and dedication of all those who have contributed to the preservation of this sacred heritage.

May the legacy of Nityanand Bhagwan and the temples continue to shine as beacons of spiritual light, guiding all who seek peace, wisdom, and divine grace.

The experience of writing about Dada's journey was soul-satisfying for me.

The whole family of Shri Babubhai Hargovindas Mehta was blessed by Nityanand Bhagwan, Shri Jananand Baba, and Shri Ghadge Maharaj.

The family of Shri Navnit Babubhai Mehta personally feels blessed and knows that divine presence is always there with our family.

Jai Nityanand !!!

ॐ सर्वे भवन्तु सुखिनः

सर्वे सन्तु निरामयाः।

सर्वे भद्राणि पश्यन्तु मा कश्चिद्दःखभाग्भवेत।

ॐ शान्तिः शान्तिः शान्तिः॥

May God's Blessings always be with you All.

"SHREE JAGADGURU NITYANAND BHAGWAN KI JAI"

"SHREE PARAMPUJYA JANANAD SWAMI KI JAI"

Nityananda Bhagwan ki Aarti;

Jai Jai Aarti Nityananda, Saguna Rupi Govinda (2) Jai Jai Aarti Nityananda,

Pratham Datta Rupa Ghesi

Dwitiya Shripada Hoshi

Tritiya Narahari Hoshi

Ganagapuri Lilaa Daavishi

Jai Jai Aarti Nityananda, Saguna Rupi Govinda (2) Jai Jai Aarti Nityananda

Maanik Prabhu Tu Hoshi

Akkalkot Swami Hoshi

Shirdi Sai Nath Hoshi

Kaliyugi Nityananda Banashi

Jai Jai Aarti Nityananda, Saguna Rupi Govinda (2) Jai Jai Aarti Nityananda,

Aaisi Aneka Rupe Tu Ghesi

Ganeshpuri Tu Vasashi

Bhaktanchi Iccha Puravishi

Balanna Bahu Aavadashi

Jai Jai Aarti Nityananda, Saguna Rupi Govinda, Jai Jai Aarti Nityananda.

Photo Gallery

Om Nityananda

BABUBHAI HARGOVINDDAS MEHTA (LOKHANDWALA)   VIMLABEN BABUBHAI MEHTA (LOKHANDWALA)
13.1.1919 - 21.12.1986   1.1.1923- 16.9.2000

Om Nityananda

IN THE EARLY DAYS

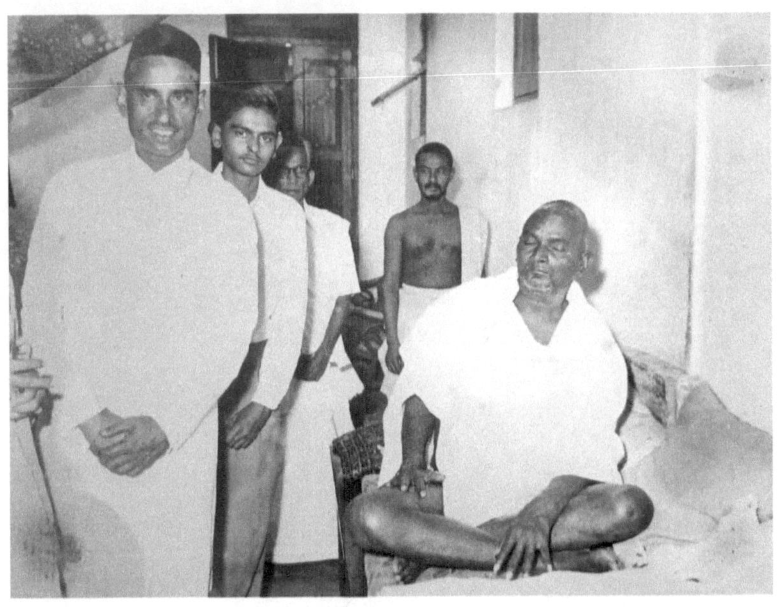

*Shri Babubhai H Mehta (Lokhandwala) with his elder son Navnit Mehta in presence of Bhagwan Nityanand at **Ganeshpuri***

Om Nityananda

Nityanand Baba sitting in **Kailash building** surround by devotees - Shri Babubhai Lokhandwala 10th from right, Navnit Mehta 9th from right, Bhoja Shetty 11th from right and Swami Muktanand 2nd from right with Nityanand Baba

Om Nityananda

Younger son Arvind Mehta, Babubhai Lokhandwala,
elder son Navnit Mehta and Shri Silam in **Ganeshpuri**

Om Nityananda

Nityanand Baba walking on the terrace of **Kailash building** in Ganeshpuri and Smt. Vimlaben Mehta & children of her family with other devotees taking darshan of the Enlightened One

Om Nityananda

Das Avtaar's Journey To Kanhangad

Das Avatar's journey to Kanhangad on a steamer - One can see Shankar Rao, Babubhai Lokhandwala, Maneklal Zaveri, Muktanand Swami with others

Om Nityananda

Jananand Baba and Shri Babubhai Lokhandwala in Kanhangad during **Das Avtaar** trip

Om Nityananda

Swami Muktanand with Babubhai Lokhandwala in
Kanhangad during the **Das Avtaar** trip

Om Nityananda

Kanhangad Mandir

In the early days of Kanhangad temple construction – 1962

Om Nityananda

Nityanand Baba's Murti taken in a large wooden box aboard a steamer
ship from Mumbai port to Mangalore port in 1963

Om Nityananda

Nityanand Baba's Murti arriving at Kanhangad ashram.
The entrance to the ashram looked like this in 1963.

Om Nityananda

The wooden box with Nityanand Baba's murti arrives outside Kanhangad ashram. Jananand Baba removing the garlands before opening the box.

Om Nityananda

Shri Babubhai Lokhandwala, Smt. Vimlaben and Mother Maniben Mehta on the truck with Nityanand Baba's murti in the background being taken in Kanhangad town for people to have darshan.

Om Nityananda

Programme

Saturday	27–4–63	Sri Ganesh Sthapan, Navagraha Pooja Japa & Kumbabhishekam.
Sunday	28–4–63	Homa, Havan and Yagna Vidhi etc.
		Evening :—Public Meeting.
		Night :—Bhajan & Variety Entertainment.
Monday	29–4–63	Pranaprathistha of the Murti of Bhagwan Sri Nityananda and Opening Ceremony of the Bhagwan's Temple by Shri M. S. Kannamwar.
		Prasadam Bhandara.

' Om Namo Nityanandaya '

The Pranapratishtha Mahotsava of the Murti of

BHAGWAN · SRI NITYANANDA

and the opening ceremony of the Bhagwan's Temple by

Shri M. S. KANNAMWAR, CHIEF MINISTER, MAHARASHTRA STATE

will take place in the Holy presence of SWAMI JANANANDJI

at Shri Nityananda Ashram, Kanhangad (Kerala State) on the 29th April, 1963,

Shri R. SANKER, CHIEF MINISTER, KERALA STATE

has also kindly agreed to participate in the function.

You are cordially invited to this auspicious function with family and friends.

R. S. V. P.
BABUBHAI H. MEHTA
C/O. SHRI NITYANANDA ASHRAM,
KANHANGAD [KERALA STATE]

BABUBHAI H. MEHTA
BHAGWANDAS H. MEHTA
DHIRAJLAL N. GORADIA

The Invitation to come to Pranprathistha Mohotsav of the Murti of Bhagwan Shri Nityanand and the opening ceremony of the Bhagwan's temple on 29th April 1963

Om Nityananda

Murtikar Shri Ganesh Patkar and Jananand Swami with Nityanand Baba's murti kept in the Gopuram, Kanhangad

Om Nityananda

Shri Babubhai Lokhandwala sitting at the feet of the murti and Smt. Vimlaben Mehta standing near Bhagwan inside the Gopuram at Kanhangad

Om Nityananda

Ganesh Patkar ji during Pranprathistha of Kanhangad temple

Om Nityananda

In 1963 Shri Babubhai Lokhandwala on the top of
the Kanhangad temple during the Kalash and
Dhwaja Dand pooja and installation

Om Nityananda

Welcome gate was built in Kanhangad in 1963

Om Nityananda

Long shot of Nityanand Ashram Kanhangad in 1963

Om Nityananda

Shri Babubhai Lokhandwala with Smt. Vimlaben Mehta and their daughter Niranjana Mehta in Kanhangad temple in 1963 during Pranprathistha Havan

Om Nityananda

Navnit Mehta, Babubhai Lokhandwala, Arvind Mehta, Vimlaben
Mehta and Niranjana Mehta in Kanhangad
mandir's Pranprathistha havan in 1963

Om Nityananda

Shri Babubhai Lokhandwala and Smt. Vimlaben Mehta at
Kanhangad mandir in 1963

Om Nityananda

Shri Prabhashankar Sompura and
Shri Babubhai Lokhandwala inside the Garbha Grih of
Nityanand Baba temple, Kanhangad

Om Nityananda

Chief Minister of Maharashtra Shri Kannamwar and Chief Minister of Kerala Shri R Sankar in Kanhangad on Pranprathistha day in 1963.

Om Nityananda

Jananand Baba with Chief Minister of Maharashtra Shri Kannamwar in Kanhangad, 1963.

Om Nityananda

Jananand Baba sharing his views with Baburao Khade and
Babubhai Lokhandwala

Om Nityananda

Mountain of rice.
Babubhai Lokhandwala and Vimlaben offering flowers to
Annapurna Maa in Kanhangad kitchen in 1963

Om Nityananda

Jananand Swami during Pranprathistha of
Kanhangad temple

Om Nityananda

Shri Babubhai Hargovindas Mehta (Lokhandwala) in
Kanhangad in 1980s

Om Nityananda

Akeri Ekeri Bateri Baba in white marble and
the pink marble paduka with bhagwan's footprints
in Kanhangad temple

Om Nityananda

Kanhangad temple - Present Day

Om Nityananda

Guruvan Temple

In the early days of construction of Guruvan temple
Shri Babubhai Lokhandwala and Smt. Vimlaben

Om Nityananda

From right to left – Shri Sompuraji, Nityanand Baba's murti, Babubhai Lokhandwala, elder son Navnit Mehta, wife Vimlaben Mehta, son Arvind Mehta & daughter Niranjana Mehta in Guruvan mandir's Pranprathistha havan in 1965

Om Nityananda

Jananand Swami inspecting the Pranprathistha ceremony of Guruvan temple and Shri Babubhai Lokhandwala and Smt. Vimlaben performing the havan ceremony

Om Nityananda

Shri Sompuraji, Shri Babubhai Lokhandwala, and
Smt. Vimlaben in Guruvan during the Pranprathistha of
the Murti in 1965

Om Nityananda

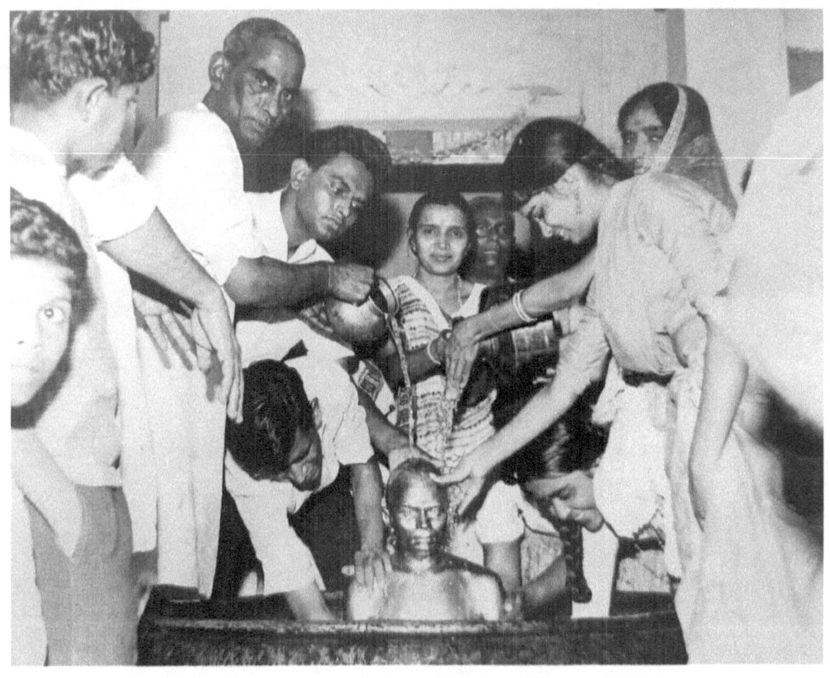

In 1965, during Abhishek of Guruvan's murti – from left to right – Shri Babubhai Lokhandwala, Navnit Mehta, cousin, Vimlaben and Niranjana Mehta

Om Nityananda

In Guruvan – Doing Abhishek of Dhwaja Dand and Om symbol –
from right to left – Niranjana Mehta, Shri Babubhai Lokhandwala,
Smt. Vimlaben Mehta, Cousin and Navnit Mehta

Om Nityananda

After the pooja of the Kalash of Guruvan temple – from right to left Niranjana Mehta, Babubhai Lokhandwala, two cousins, Smt. Vimlaben Mehta, Navnit Mehta, Arvind Menta, Sompura ji and MLA Shri Rane standing down.

Om Nityananda

Lokhandwala family on the top of Guruvan temple before
the Kalash pooja

Om Nityananda

During Pranprathishtha havan in Guruvan: Niranjana Mehta,
Smt. Vimlaben, Navnit Mehta, Shri. Babubhai Lokhandwala and
Arvind Mehta

Om Nityananda

Nityanand Baba young age murti at Guruvan temple

Om Nityananda

After the Pranprathistha ceremony in
Guruvan Shri Babubhai Lokhandwala was facilitated
by the Lt. Governor of Pondicherry Shri Silam and
Maharashtra MLA Shri Rane in 1965.

Om Nityananda

On the mic is Shri Ravindran, Navnit Mehta, Shri Babubhai Lokhandwala in Guruvan along with Lt. Governor of Pondicherry Shri Silam and his wife in 1965.

Om Nityananda

An elephant was decorated and brought by
the local devotees during the Pranprathishtha
ceremony of Guruvan temple.

Om Nityananda

Original Guruvan temple till 2009

Om Nityananda

Garbha Griha of the original Guruvan temple with Murti

Om Nityananda

Shir Malahvir swami's swords in Guruvan temple

Om Nityananda

Jananand Swami in Guruvan with
Shri Babubhai Lokhandwala and Smt. Vimlaben Mehta.

Om Nityananda

JANANAND BABA

Jananand Baba's Tulabhar completed – (from left to right) Shir Thakurbhai, Shri Krishna Nair, Jananand Baba, Navnit Mehta, Keval Mehta, Smt. Vimlaben, Shri Babubhai Lokhandwala, Hingwala, Shri Merchantbhai (sitting) Shri Chetan Patil (standing down) with Old Bhattji of Nityanand temple and Dr. Sarmistha devi in the far right.

Om Nityananda

During Tulabhar of Jananand Baba in Kanhangad: from left to right – Shri Krishna Nair, Jananand Baba, Navnit Mehta, where Babubhai Lokhandwala, Arvind Mehta and Vimlaben pouring 1/- rupee coins in the bucket with old Bhatt ji and Dipali Mehta standing down

Om Nityananda

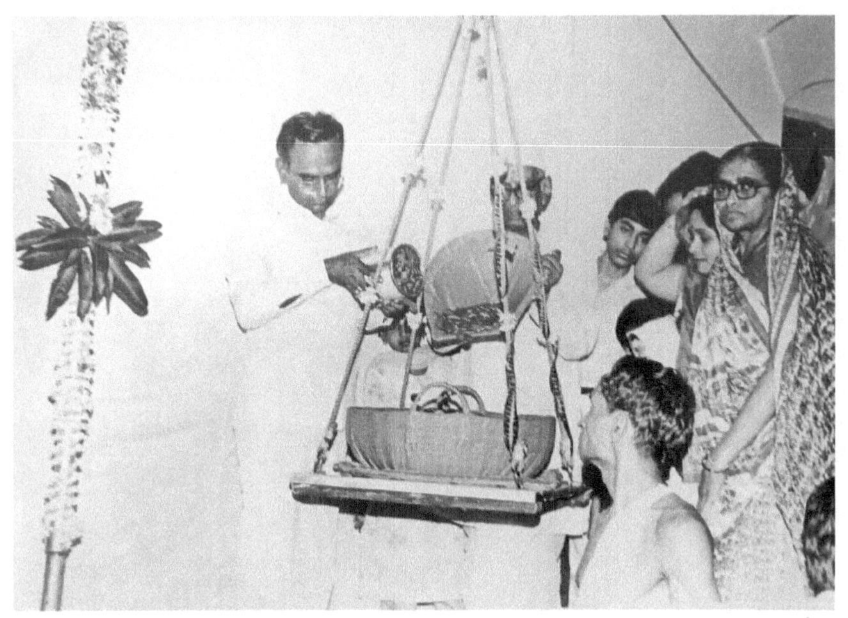

Shri Navnit Mehta and
Shri Babubhai Lokhandwala pouring 1/- rupee coins
in the bucket

Om Nityananda

Jananand Baba wearing a beautiful garland made of 1/- rupee coins
made by Lokhandwala family during the Tulabhar.

Om Nityananda

Smt. Vimlaben Mehta,
Babubhai Lokhandwala sitting with
Jananand Swami Navnit Mehta is standing and his
wife Smt. Jayshree Mehta with both their sons Monesh
and Keval sitting at Jananand Baba's feet.

Om Nityananda

During Pranprathishtha day of Kanhangad temple in 1977.
From left to right - Shri Babubhai Lokhandwala and
his family Smt. Vimlaben Mehta, Shri Navnit Mehta,
Smt. Jayshree Mehta carrying Keval Mehta and
Monesh Mehta standing down.
In the background Shri Arvind Mehta,
his wife Smt. Dharmistha Mehta carrying their
daughter Dipali Mehta and other devotees.

Om Nityananda

Dada and me in Kanhangad ashram
Jananand Baba's Samadhi mandir under construction
in the background

Om Nityananda

Top view of Jananand swami's samadhi temple
in Kanhangad

Om Nityananda

Swami Jananand Baba's Samadhi mandir murti

Om Nityananda

Jananand Baba's seat in Kanhangad ashram hall

Om Nityananda

From left to right: Dasa (Gurudasan M),
Thamban (Ratheesh B R) (Meenakshi Amma's son),
Suku (Sukumaran N) and Gangu (Gangadhara A K)
These men are in their late 50s, and they are amongst
many who have served Jananand Baba and
the ashram since their childhood

Om Nityananda

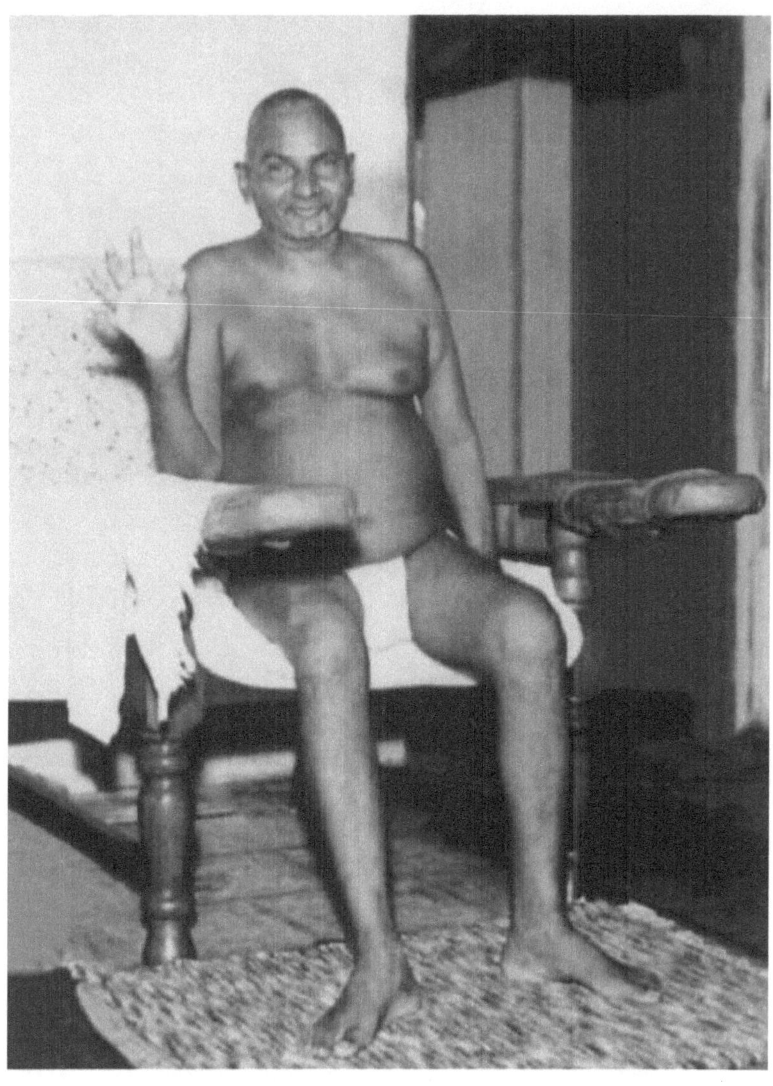

Nityanand Baba in Kailash building in Ganeshpuri

Om Nityananda

Babubhai Lokhandwala offering
Panchamrut abhishek to Nityanand Baba on his
samadhi in Ganeshpuri Mandir

Om Nityananda

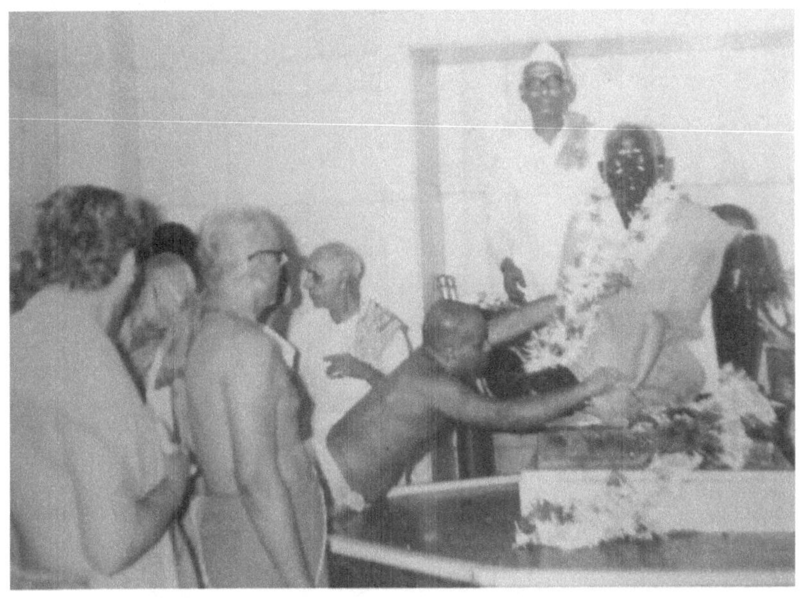

Babubhai Lokhandwala offering garland to
Nityanand Baba's samadhi in Ganeshpuri temple.
Gopalmama also seen

Om Nityananda

The marble tablet inside the Ganeshpuri's Samadhi temple where the name of the founder trustees are mentioned.

No. 8 is Babubhai H. Mehta (Lokhandwala)

Om Nityananda

Shri Navnit Babubhai Mehta and Smt. Jayshree Navnit Mehta

Om Nityananda